# Profiles in American History

*The Life and Times of*

# JOHN HANCOCK

## Mitchell Lane
### PUBLISHERS

P.O. Box 196 · Hockessin, Delaware 19707

# Titles in the Series

*The Life and Times of*

# JOHN HANCOCK

Marylou Morano Kjelle

Printing        1        2        3        4        5        6        7        8        9

Library of Congress Cataloging-in-Publication Data
Kjelle, Marylou Morano.
   The life and times of John Hancock / by Marylou Morano Kjelle.
      p. cm. — (Profiles in American history)
   Includes bibliographical references and index.
   ISBN 1-58415-443-8 (library bound)
   1. Hancock, John, 1737–1793—Juvenile literature. 2. Statesmen—United States—Biography—Juvenile literature. 3. United States. Declaration of Independence—Signers—Biography—Juvenile literature. 4. Governors—Massachusetts—Biography—Juvenile literature. I. Title. II. Series.
E302.6.H23K47 2007
973.3'092—dc22                                        2006006108

ISBN-10: 1-58415-443-8                     ISBN-13: 9781584154433

**ABOUT THE AUTHOR:** Marylou Morano Kjelle is a freelance writer and photo-journalist who lives and works in central New Jersey. She is a regular contributor to several local newspaper and online publications. She has written over 30 nonfiction books for young readers, including *Brittany Murphy, Jesse McCartney, Francis Scott Key, Jacques Cartier,* and *Extreme Skateboarding with Paul Rodriguez Jr.* for Mitchell Lane Publishers. Marylou has a master's of science degree from Rutgers University. She teaches English and writing at Rutgers and several other colleges in New Jersey.

**PHOTO CREDITS:** pp. 6, 8, 10, 18, 20, 29, 30, 34—Library of Congress.

# Profiles in American History

# Contents

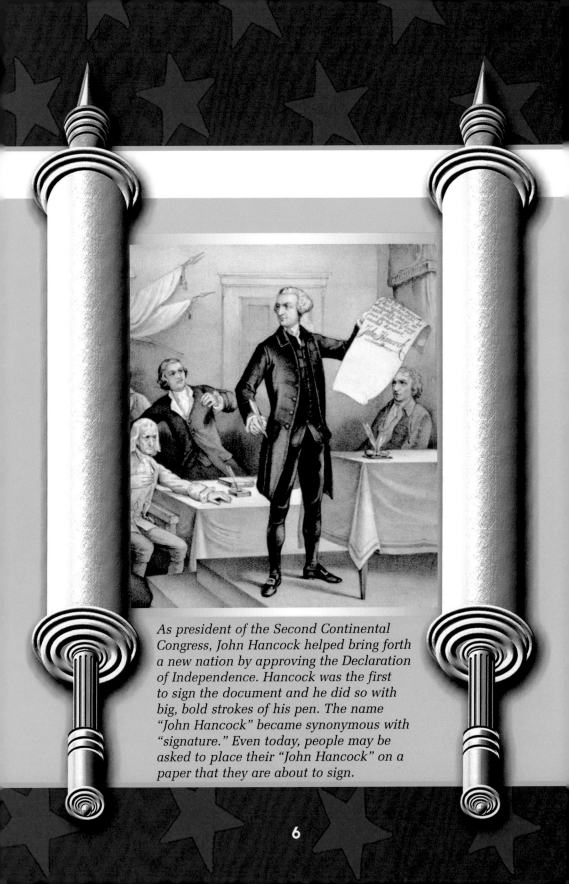

As president of the Second Continental Congress, John Hancock helped bring forth a new nation by approving the Declaration of Independence. Hancock was the first to sign the document and he did so with big, bold strokes of his pen. The name "John Hancock" became synonymous with "signature." Even today, people may be asked to place their "John Hancock" on a paper that they are about to sign.

# CHAPTER 1

## A Nation Is Born

Silence fell over the white-paneled room of the Pennsylvania State House on July 4, 1776, as John Hancock stared at the document placed before him. Then he stretched out his arm and, with a quick flourish, boldly signed his name at the bottom. As the president of the Second Continental Congress, Hancock was the first to sign the newly adopted Declaration of Independence. The members of Congress who witnessed Hancock's signature were aware, to a man, of how serious the moment was. Hancock glanced around the room at the solemn faces before him and reflected on everything that had brought them to this historic moment.

In September 1774, after a decade of unfair taxation, the First Continental Congress had been called to address King George III's unjust policies toward the colonies. Those present had been hopeful that the king would recognize the rights of the American colonies. Even though they didn't agree with the king's treatment of the colonies, the delegates still considered themselves Englishmen and loyal subjects. They wanted to live in peace with their mother country.

But matters had taken another turn. A skirmish between British soldiers, or "redcoats," and the minutemen at Lexington and Concord, Massachusetts, in April 1775 had developed into the War for Independence. The Second Continental Congress had come together a few weeks later. By this time it was clear that the only course of action was to become independent from England. For over

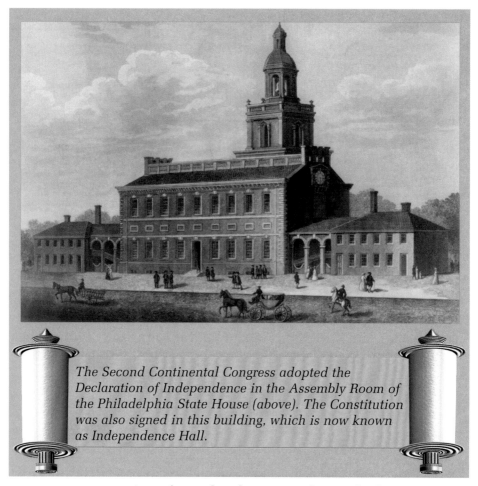

*The Second Continental Congress adopted the Declaration of Independence in the Assembly Room of the Philadelphia State House (above). The Constitution was also signed in this building, which is now known as Independence Hall.*

a year, representatives from the thirteen colonies had met, almost daily, to work toward bringing forth a new nation. A continental army had been formed, and the Virginian George Washington had been named its commander in chief. As the weeks turned into months, the American colonies began to look less like loyal British subjects and more like independent American states.

Before the colonies could claim complete independence, however, a declaration had to be made in writing. Another delegate from Virginia, Thomas Jefferson, and a few other members of Congress had been asked to draw up a document that declared the thirteen colonies free and independent. Jefferson spent two weeks drafting the declaration, which he called *A Declaration by the Representatives*

*of the United States of America, in General Congress Assembled.* When it was first presented to the full congress, the delegates had suggested more than thirty changes. Jefferson made the changes and presented a revised draft to the congress on June 28, 1776.

Hancock was sure that Congress would not adjourn before the delegates had voted on the matter of independence. He scheduled a debate on the declaration for July 2. Before the delegates began their discussion, Hancock asked that a "trial" vote be taken. Were the colonies ready to unanimously declare independence? One by one the delegates of each colony stated the wishes of the people they represented. Twelve colonies voted to separate from England and declare "independency." The delegates of the thirteenth colony, New York, weren't sure how their people wanted them to vote, so they abstained. Instructions to vote in favor of independence would not reach them until July 15, almost two weeks later.

With a unanimous decision behind them, the delegates moved forward with the creation of a new nation. On July 3, Hancock asked Congress to again study the declaration. Congress suggested more changes. The debate over wording lasted into the night of July 3 and continued for most of July 4. A few more changes were easily made here and there. Other parts of the declaration, however—those mostly having to do with the issue of slavery—continued to be a source of argument. Eventually these sections were removed. By the evening of July 4, Congress had come to an agreement on the revised version of the Declaration of Independence and had given it to Hancock to sign.

The next day, copies of the declaration were printed and carried by post riders to all thirteen states. One copy was sent to General Washington to read to the troops. Wherever it was heard, the news of independence was celebrated by bell ringing, fireworks, and bonfires.

John Hancock and Secretary Charles Thomson were the only members of Congress to sign the Declaration of Independence on July 4, 1776. A few weeks later a parchment copy, which all the delegates would sign, was ready. On August 2, Congress once again met in the Pennsylvania State House. Approaching a table in delegations by state, one by one the delegates signed the "The Unanimous Declaration of the Thirteen United States of America." Each man knew that he was committing an act of treason by signing. If the War

Thomas Jefferson is considered to be the primary author of the Declaration of Independence, but other delegates gave him input. Those who helped Jefferson (far left) were (left to right) John Adams, Benjamin Franklin, Robert Livingston, and Roger Sherman.

for Independence were lost, each would surely pay with his life. There would be no leniency for any man who signed a document announcing a break from England.

There would especially be no leniency for John Hancock. The British considered Hancock one of the most rebellious of the Patriot leaders and had offered 500 pounds for his capture. After placing his bold signature on the Declaration of Independence for the second time, Hancock turned to the other members of the Continental Congress and said: "I write so George III may read without his spectacles. Now he can double the reward of 500 pounds on my head."[1]

It is also believed that Hancock told the delegates of the Second Continental Congress, "We must be unanimous. There must be no pulling different ways; we must all hang together."[2]

"Yes, we must, indeed, all hang together, or . . . we shall [surely] all hang separately," Benjamin Franklin is said to have answered.[3]

By placing their signatures on the Declaration of Independence, the signers freed the thirteen colonies from the tyranny of England. They had entered the State House earlier that day as British subjects. It was as Americans—led by John Hancock—that they left.

# The First Continental Congress

*The First Continental Congress*

The First Continental Congress was held on September 5, 1774, in Philadelphia's Carpenters' Hall. Fifty-five delegates from twelve of the thirteen colonies were present at this meeting; Georgia was the only colony that didn't send representation. The First Continental Congress was called to protest a series of unjust laws that had been passed by England during the 1760s and early part of the 1770s. One of the laws closed Boston Harbor, leaving its citizens facing the prospect of starvation. Those attending the First Continental Congress considered themselves loyal subjects of King George III. Unfair treatment by England, however, was quickly bringing the colonies together as one united nation. Many of the delegates to the First Continental Congress, including George Washington, John Adams, John Jay, and Patrick Henry, went on to become the Founding Fathers and future leaders of the United States of America.

At the First Continental Congress, the delegates drew up and sent a petition, which they called "A Declaration of Rights and Grievances," to the king. The petition asked that the unfair laws be repealed. The congress also debated the creation of an American Parliament, and called for the formation of an association that would oversee colonial boycotts of English products.

The First Continental Congress was in session until October 26, 1774. Before closing, the delegates realized there would most likely be a need to call additional Continental Congresses

*The Second Continental Congress*

in the future. They decided to come together again in 1775 if King George III did not address their concerns. In May 1775, the Second Continental Congress was called. At this meeting were three men who had been absent from the first Congress—Benjamin Franklin, Thomas Jefferson, and John Hancock.

For Your Information

who lived half a world away? Didn't the colonists have the right to govern themselves? These questions, and others like them, were beginning to be heard throughout all thirteen colonies, but the people of Massachusetts seemed to be asking them the loudest and the most often.

This was the Massachusetts into which John Hancock was born on January 12, 1737. He was born in Braintree (now called Quincy), a small town south of Boston. John's father, the Reverend John Hancock, was a Puritan minister, and his father, John's grandfather, was a minister as well. Reverend Hancock had studied to be a minister at Harvard University. In 1726 he moved to Braintree and became the pastor of the town's North Parish.

A few years later, Reverend Hancock met Mary Hawke Thaxter. She was a widow, and nine years younger than he was. They were married on December 13, 1733. About two years later, their first child, a daughter, Mary, was born. A son, whom they named John after his father and grandfather, was born next. Four years later, another son, Ebenezer, was born.

John's early childhood years were happy ones. He had many playmates; one of his closest was John Adams, who was the son of a farmer. The boys explored the fields and swamps around Braintree. They flew kites in the summer and went sledding in the winter. In colonial times, children sometimes attended a dame school, a school run by an older woman in her home. When he was six years old, John started classes at the home of Dame Belcher. In the evenings, after a day of school and play, John felt secure in the warmth of the family that awaited him back home in the manse. There, with their father nearby if they needed him, the Hancock children would continue their lessons.

Life did not stay warm and cozy for young John Hancock for long. In 1744, when he was seven years old, his father became sick. Soon after, he died, and John lost not only his father, but his home as well. The Hancock family could no longer live in the manse, for it was to be given to the new pastor. With three children and no home to give them, Mrs. Hancock had only one option: She had to separate the family. John was sent to Boston to live with his father's brother, Thomas, who was a businessman. Mrs. Hancock, Mary, and Ebenezer moved to Lexington, into the manse with Grandmother and Grandfather Hancock.

John's uncle Thomas was one of the wealthiest men in Boston. He had started in business at the age of fourteen as an apprentice to a bookseller. Over the years the business had grown to include several shops, many ships, and a warehouse on Long Warf. He exported whale oil and whale bones, and imported ribbons and other luxuries. His many trading ships crisscrossed the ocean from Boston to England, and carried supplies south to the West Indies and north to Newfoundland.

A well-respected businessman, Thomas had been elected selectman, the town's highest office. He was also a member of a branch of the Massachusetts legislature called the General Council.

Uncle Thomas and his wife, Aunt Lydia, lived in a mansion in Beacon Hill, a wealthy area of Boston. Compared to the manse in Braintree, Uncle Thomas's home was magnificent. It sat on a large piece of land surrounded by beautiful gardens. It was made of the finest granite. Its fifty windows looked out over Boston Harbor and the Boston Commons, a large park open to the public. People held meetings at the Commons, played there, and let their livestock graze there. To celebrate happy occasions, the people of Boston lit bonfires and fireworks on the Commons. From his bedroom window, John could see everything going on there.

Thomas and Lydia had no children of their own. They welcomed young John into their home and treated him like a son. Over time, John came to think of Uncle Thomas and Aunt Lydia as his parents. As the years passed, his mother would marry once again, and he would see less and less of her and his sister, Mary. Years later, when he heard Mary had become engaged to be married, he sent her a letter. "I hope you will give me an Invitation," he wrote.[1] He did, however, keep in contact with Ebenezer.

Uncle Thomas and Aunt Lydia enrolled John in the Boston Latin School, the first American public school and one of the best schools in Boston. (Benjamin Franklin and Samuel Adams, two other American Patriots, also attended the Boston Latin School.) The students studied Greek, Latin, and penmanship. Dame Belcher had taught John well. He was found to be ahead of his class, and was skipped to the third year. It was at Boston Latin that John learned to write his name in the grand style he used to sign the Declaration of Independence.

By 1750, John had completed his studies at Boston Latin School and was ready to take his entrance exam for Harvard University. He was questioned by Harvard's President Edward Holyoke and four tutors. He had to answer all the questions in Latin. In addition, he was asked to translate passages from English into Latin and Greek. He passed the entrance exam, and at thirteen and a half years old, he became the second youngest in his class of twenty students. Today, thirteen is a very young age to attend college. Back when John was growing up, however, students did not attend a high school. They went directly to college after finishing grammar school.

The pace at Harvard was grueling. John was up before sunrise to attend morning prayers. Then he ate a light breakfast of milk with a biscuit or slice of bread. Lecture began promptly at eight, and the rest of the morning was spent studying Greek, Latin, rhetoric, astronomy, several different types of mathematics, and physics. His noon meal usually was some type of meat and a mug of cider. Then there was more study until evening prayers at five o'clock. Supper was at seven-thirty, and at nine all the students went to their rooms for the night. A student received a heavy fine if he was late for meals or lecture. As the nephew of a wealthy merchant, a fine did not discourage John. For more serious misbehaviors, especially those that involved drinking, a student might be "degraded," or reduced in class position. Harvard records show that John and Samuel Quincy, his friend from Braintree, were both fined and degraded several times.

Also attending Harvard with John was another boyhood friend, John Adams. Adams and Hancock were two very different young men. Adams was studious and somber, while Hancock was a more sociable fellow who didn't take his studies as seriously as his friend. Hancock also had a great need to be liked and admired by his peers. Spending so much time with friends reflected on his grades and often got him in trouble.

Despite his casual attitude toward his studies, Hancock graduated from Harvard University in July 1754. Besides Aunt Lydia and Uncle Thomas, John's mother, sister, and brother also came to see him graduate. The ceremony lasted four hours and was followed by a feast hosted by the graduates.

John was seventeen years old. Four years of Harvard were behind him. Both for John and for the thirteen colonies, challenging times lay ahead.

# Harvard University

Like his father before him, John Hancock attended Harvard University. Harvard is the oldest college in the United States. It was founded in 1636 by Massachusetts colonists, mostly Puritans, who had been educated in England at Oxford and Cambridge universities. These men wanted their sons to have an education equal to theirs, and they petitioned the Massachusetts legislature for the funds to start an institute of higher learning in their colony. The General Court of Massachusetts provided the initial amount of 400 pounds to start a college. The city of Newtowne, later renamed Cambridge, was chosen as the site of the school. An acre of land with one house sitting upon it served as Harvard's first campus.

In 1638, John Harvard, a young minister living in a nearby town who was dying of tuberculosis, heard about the college. He left the school his entire library of 400 books, plus half his money—about 800 pounds. Shortly thereafter, the General Court ordered the college named Harvard College in honor of the minister.

In 1640, Harvard College's first freshman class had four students and one professor, who also served as college president. Later, tutors were responsible for incoming classes, and one tutor would teach one class all subjects for four years. All students studied the same subjects regardless of the profession they were planning to enter.

In 1780, the state of Massachusetts officially recognized Harvard College as Harvard University. Harvard Medical School was founded during the Revolutionary War in 1782. Harvard Law School was founded in 1817, and Harvard Divinity School in 1819.

Six United States presidents—John Adams, John Quincy Adams, Theodore Roosevelt, Franklin Delano Roosevelt, John F. Kennedy, and George W. Bush—graduated from Harvard. Several other presidents either attended Harvard or were awarded honorary degrees from the university.

Thomas Pownall was an Englishman who was appointed Royal Governor of Massachusetts by William Pitt. He served from 1757 to 1760. Upon returning to England after his governorship, he became a member of Parliament, and during the war, became known for his support of the colonies.

# CHAPTER
# 3

## The Merchant Prince

After graduation, John returned home to Beacon Hill and began working for his uncle. He learned to manage one of the stores, as well as the shipping end of the business. Day after day, John studied the loading and unloading of the cargo that sailed on the ships traveling between Boston and London. He also learned how to order merchandise, advertise the business, and handle correspondence.

During this time, John changed from a college man into a business man. He was well-mannered and hardworking. He knew that if he proved himself worthy, all that Uncle Thomas owned would one day be his. Uncle Thomas's business was prospering. England was in the middle of the French and Indian War, and Uncle Thomas's company had received a contract to ship supplies to the British troops quartered in Nova Scotia.

In 1760, when John was twenty-three years old, Uncle Thomas sent his nephew to London. He wanted John to meet his business agents and to learn more about the business. "He is a sober, Modest Young Gentleman," Uncle Thomas wrote to his partners in London.[1]

John was accompanied on the trip by former Massachusetts governor Thomas Pownall, who was returning home to England. They sailed in June 1760 on the *Benjamin and Samuel*. The voyage to England took almost seven weeks. Once he arrived, John stayed at the home of one of Uncle Thomas's friends, Jonathan Bernard.

Although the main reason for the trip to London had been to represent the firm on business, the young man took the time to have some fun, too. He viewed the city as being full of "pleasurable enjoyments and tempting scenes."[2] He took in the sites, such as the River Thames and Kensington Gardens. He traveled to the cities of Bristol and Manchester. He observed Parliament in session and even saw King George II himself, at the House of Lords.

John certainly wasn't cautious when it came to spending his uncle's money. "Money some way or other goes very fast," John

*The gardens surrounding Kensington Palace and other historic buildings in London are known as Kensington Gardens. Thirty years before Hancock arrived in London, Queen Caroline, wife of George II, began making major improvements to the gardens.*

wrote to Thomas when his uncle admonished him for spending so much of it.[3]

"Be frugal of Expences, do Honor to your Country & furnish Your Mind with all wise Improvements," Thomas wrote to John.[4]

John's fun came to an end on October 25, 1760, when King George II died suddenly. All of London went into mourning for their king. Citizens wore black. Main London attractions closed, including the theater, and private parties were discouraged. "Every thing here now is very dull," John wrote to Thomas.[5] John attended George II's funeral, where he saw George III, the man who would one day call John a traitor and place a price of 500 pounds on his head.

In spite of their sadness, Londoners were also excited about the coronation of George III, the grandson of George II. The young king-to-be was loved by the people of England, and John, like most of London society, was looking forward to his crowning in April. "[I]t is the grandest thing I shall ever meet with," he wrote home.[6] But he was not to witness the coronation, which had been postponed until a wife could be found for the young king. When Aunt Lydia's father died in early 1761, John set sail for home to be with his aunt in her time of mourning.

John immersed himself in the business when he returned home. On January 1, 1763, Uncle Thomas made John his business partner. "I have this Day Taken my Nephew Mr. John Hancock, into Partnership with me," Thomas wrote to his lawyer.[7] According to Thomas, John had the qualities of "Uprightness" and "great Abilities for Business."[8] As soon as the partnership was complete, Thomas changed the name of his firm to Thomas Hancock & Company.

A short while after taking John into the business, Thomas became too sick to run the company. Soon John was managing Thomas Hancock & Company mostly on his own. The business continued to prosper, and John, with his uncle's permission, negotiated contracts to ship whale oil between Nantucket and London.

In August 1764, Uncle Thomas collapsed while he was on his way to attend a meeting of the Governor's Council at the State House. He was carried back to his home, where he died later that day. John was twenty-seven years old, and from his uncle he inherited Thomas Hancock & Company, which included full warehouses and stores on the Boston waterfront as well as real estate throughout New England.

King George III (left) succeeded his grandfather, King George II, to the throne in 1760 and reigned for sixty years. Although he was one of the longest reigning British kings, he was among the most unpopular.

All totaled, Uncle Thomas left John an estate of 70,000 pounds, which today would be equal to several million dollars. His inheritance made John the richest man in Massachusetts and the second richest in the colonies.

Like his uncle before him, John became a respected member of Boston society. According to John Adams, John Hancock was a "steady, punctual, industrious, indefatigable man of business . . . always genteelly dressed, according to the fashions of the day."[9] Lean and slender, Hancock stood nearly six feet tall. He had dark brown hair over which he usually wore a wig. His trousers and coats were made of velvet and satin, which he wore with lacy shirts and shoes with shiny buckles.

John's fortune and his sense of style made him a favorite with the ladies of Boston. They found him to be quite handsome, and were attracted to him as much for his aristocratic looks and warm personality as for his money. Aunt Lydia, however, kept a close eye on the

nephew she thought of as a son. She allowed him to court only the women of whom she approved.

Other than a case of gout now and then, and headaches for which no doctor was able to find a cause, Hancock was in good health. He liked making people happy. A generous man, he often paid his friends' bills when they were in debt. He gave money and stacks of firewood to the poor. He bought pews, Bibles, and windows for the churches of Boston. He gave a large collection of books to the Harvard University Library.

John helped the community in other ways. Thomas Hancock & Company provided jobs for many of Boston's citizens. John Adams once said that at least one thousand families depended on Hancock for their livelihood. Therefore, when Parliament began taxing the colonies, Hancock had many reasons to wonder how it would affect his business and those he employed.

By the mid-1760s, the mother country was sorely in need of money. There had been the costly ten-year-long French and Indian War, which England had won in 1763. Managing the thirteen colonies from half a world away was also taking its toll on the British treasury. England needed additional ways to bring in money, and taxing the colonies seemed a sensible way to do so.

In 1764, Parliament passed the Sugar Act, which enforced a tax on goods that came into the colonies from places other than England. The Sugar Act also enforced a tax on molasses. Before the Sugar Act, it was easy for merchants, including Hancock, to smuggle taxable items into the colonies from time to time. The Sugar Act called for tax officers to be present when trading ships docked at port. It was the tax officers' job to catch smugglers and to be sure taxes were paid on all goods brought into the country.

The Sugar Act angered the people of Boston, who immediately called for its repeal. For the first time, cries of "no taxation without representation" were heard. Boston's House of Representatives organized a committee of correspondence to communicate with other colonies about the Sugar Act. Thomas Hancock & Company had never faced hard times before. Now the end of the French and Indian War brought the end of the contracts to supply the soldiers, and business had begun to slow down. Because of the Sugar Act, the colonies decided to boycott cargoes from England, which reduced the number of goods to sell. To make matters worse, Boston was facing an economic depression, so most people didn't have the money to purchase what goods were available. "Times are very bad & precarious here," Hancock wrote to his business associates in London in 1764.[10] He tried to keep his business running by seeking out new sources of whale oil.

In March 1765, nearly a year after the Sugar Act was passed, Parliament passed the Stamp Act. This was another law whose aim was to generate money from the colonies. The Stamp Act required any type of paper, including newspapers, diplomas, licenses, legal papers, and notices, to have a stamp on it to show that the tax had been paid. Books, pamphlets, and playing cards were also included in the items that required a stamp. The cries of "no taxation without representation" that began with the Sugar Act got louder with the Stamp Act.

As with the Sugar Act, Hancock was also opposed to the Stamp Act. As a businessman in the colonies, he knew that any law which restricted trade in the colonies would eventually do the same in England. And as an Englishman, the taxes were even more difficult to understand. "I have a Right to the Libertys & Privileges of the English Constitution, & I as an Englishman will enjoy them," he wrote to his London partners.[11] He protested the Stamp Act openly, emphasizing, "Not a man in England in proportion to his estate, pays the tax that I do."[12]

Hancock was not the only one in Boston who was unhappy with the new taxes. A group of Boston men had begun meeting secretly to talk about England's treatment of the colonies and the unfair taxes. John joined this group, which called itself the Long Room Club because they met in a long room above the *Boston Gazette* newspaper offices. All were members of the Whig Party, which was opposed to strong monarch rule.

In 1765, Hancock followed in Thomas's footsteps and was elected a selectman for the town of Boston. A change was slowly coming over John Hancock: The Merchant Prince was becoming a politician.

## The Intolerable Acts

The British Parliament responded to the Boston Tea Party by passing a series of four acts, or laws, designed to punish the colonies, especially Massachusetts. In England, these acts were called the Punitive or Coercive Acts. In America, the colonists called them the Intolerable Acts, because they could not be tolerated.

The first Intolerable Act was the Boston Port Bill, passed in March 1774 and put into effect June 1 of the same year. The bill closed Boston Harbor and moved the capital of Massachusetts to Salem. Boston Harbor was ordered to remain closed until the colonists had reimbursed the British crown and English merchants for the tea destroyed by the Boston Tea Party.

*Boston Tea Party*

On May 20, 1774, King George III signed the Administration of Justice Act. This law gave the governor the power to move trials to other colonies or even to England. The law also gave the governor the right to call in the British Army to put down disturbances caused by the colonists. The Quartering Act, passed on June 2, 1774, applied not just to Massachusetts: It forced all American colonists to house British troops in their homes when there wasn't enough barrack space for them.

The act the colonists found the most "intolerable," however, was the Massachusetts Bay Regulating Act. With this act, the colonists of Massachusetts lost their right to elect officials and law officers. The Regulating Act granted these positions only through appointment by the king. In addition, all town meetings were banned unless first approved by the governor.

The goal of the Coercive Acts was to stop the seeds of rebellion that were beginning to sprout in the colonies, especially in Massachusetts. Instead, the Coercive Acts brought the colonies together and led to the calling of the First Continental Congress.

Samuel Adams was a fiery speaker known for his strong stance on independence for the American colonies. He was among the first to call for a meeting of representatives of the colonies to address grievances with England. He served in both the First and Second Continental Congresses, and later as governor of Massachusetts.

# CHAPTER
# 4

## Rebel Ringleader

As soon as news of the Stamp Act reached Boston, groups of citizens began planning ways to resist it. One group, called the Sons of Liberty, actively protested the tax. The Sons of Liberty was first organized in New York City and Connecticut in 1765, then spread to the other colonies. The group organized mobs of colonists and sent them to harass the officers the king who were put in charge of enforcing the Stamp Act. Many of the officers resigned rather than face the anger of the people.

John Hancock became one of the Sons of Liberty, and they were happy to have him. His money helped them, but he was more to the group than a blank check. As an important citizen of Boston and a rich merchant, he gave the organization credibility. Having someone like Hancock on their side helped the Sons of Liberty with their causes.

One of the leaders of the Sons of Liberty in Massachusetts was Samuel Adams, Hancock's friend and John Adams's cousin. Samuel was not one of the original members of the Sons of Liberty, but he had quickly assumed control of the group. Although he was Harvard-educated, Samuel was often out of work. His father had been a merchant who had lost all his money in a foolish scheme and had died bankrupt. At times it seemed as though Samuel was heading along the same path. However, once he joined the Sons of

Liberty, it was clear that Samuel's talent was not in business, but in politics.

Samuel Adams was fourteen years older than John Hancock. In many ways, the two men were opposites. Hancock was a stylish dresser, while Adams wore the plain dress of a Puritan. Hancock had plenty of money; Adams was often in debt. Hancock was a sharp businessman; Adams was a good politician. The one thing that the two men did have in common was a passion against injustice of any kind.

Before the Stamp Act went into effect on November 1, 1765, the citizens of Boston began their protests. A stuffed effigy representing Andrew Oliver, the man appointed Boston's stamp master by the king, was hung from a tree in the center of town. Then the crowd destroyed a small building on a dock that was to serve as the Stamp Office. Next the crowd destroyed Oliver's home. He resigned his position as stamp master the next day. A few nights later, the mob turned to the home of the lieutenant governor, Thomas Hutchinson. When they heard that Governor Hutchinson wasn't home, the crowd dispersed.

Hancock did not get involved with the mobs that protested the Stamp Act with destruction. Instead, he chose to fight the tax by writing to his contacts in England. In his letters, he begged them to ask Parliament to repeal the Stamp Act.

When the first shipment of stamps arrived from England, the Sons of Liberty seized them before they could be used. Hancock was determined not to do business "under a stamp." He called the Stamp Act a "cruel, grievous and inhuman act,"[1] and told Massachusetts Governor Francis Bernard that if he had to, he would sell his stock and close his warehouse doors. "I have come to a serious Resolution not to send one Ship more to sea nor to have any kind of Connection in Business under a Stamp," Hancock wrote.[2] Other Boston merchants, as well as merchants throughout the colonies, agreed with him. A boycott of British goods was organized. Colonial ships stopped sailing to London, and trade with England came to a stop.

News of Boston's protests spread quickly to the other colonies. In October 1765, a Stamp Act Congress was held in New York. Delegates from the colonies worked out a plan to help them stand fast against the Stamp Act. They published a decree that stated the

*England's Parliament has met in the Palace of Westminster since around 1530. The clock tower that houses Big Ben (on the right) was completed in 1858, nearly 100 years after Hancock's visit.*

colonists were entitled to the rights of Englishmen, including the right to decide matters concerning their taxes.

As the boycott progressed, workers and tradesmen on both continents were put out of work. Even people living in England began to pressure Parliament to remove the stamp tax. Afraid that riots might break out in London, Parliament repealed the Stamp Act in May of 1766. However, on the same day it repealed the Stamp Act, Parliament passed the Declaratory Act, which gave it the right to pass tax laws on the colonies in the future.

When news reached Boston that the stamp tax had been repealed, the entire city celebrated. Church bells rang, parades were held, and the Boston militia discharged their guns. Hancock gave the town a

*When the Stamp Act was repealed on May 1, 1766, colonists marked the occasion by holding funerals for the stamp. Artist Benjamin Wilson captured the sentiments of the colonists in this cartoon,* The Repeal, or the Funeral of Miss Anne Stamp.

display of fireworks that he shot off from the grounds of his own home. He hosted a feast for his neighbors and other important people, including Governor Bernard. For the common folk, he sent cases of wine to the Commons. A local newspaper reported that Hancock "gave a grand and elegant entertainment to the genteel part of the town, and treated the populace with a pipe of Madeira."[3] Like all Bostonians, Hancock hoped that the end of the Stamp Act would bring the beginning of peace to the city of Boston, the colony of Massachusetts, and her twelve sister colonies.

"I hope now peace & harmony will prevail, My best Influence & endeavors to that purpose will be used," Hancock wrote to his friends in London.[4]

Massachusetts, being a charter colony, was allowed to elect its own legislature. In May 1766, Hancock was elected to the Massachusetts

House of Representatives. His election was a boon for the Sons of Liberty. When Samuel Adams heard that Hancock had been elected, he said to his cousin John Adams, "The town has done a wise thing today. They have made that young man's fortune their own."5

Between running his stores, attending to his ships, and representing the people of Boston in the House of Representatives, Hancock found he hardly had time to sleep. Before long, there were more taxes to deal with. In 1767, England passed the Townshend Acts, named after Prime Minister Charles Townshend, who convinced Parliament to pass them. They taxed glass, paper, paint, lead, and tea imported by the colonies. In addition, the Townshend Acts called for special tax agents to be sent from England to Boston. Their job was to board ships after they came into port with their goods. Like the Sugar Act, the tax agents would see to it that all taxes were paid.

Once again Boston protested the unfair taxation without representation. At a meeting of the House of Representatives, Hancock formally denounced the Townshend Acts when he declared he would not allow tax officers to board any of his ships returning from London. A short time later, he had an opportunity to prove his mettle. When his boat *Lydia* returned from London on April 7, 1768, two tax officers boarded the vessel. Hancock was called and he rushed to his ship, demanding to see their authorization. The officers did not have a special search warrant, called a writ of assistance. Hancock told the tax officers that they could stay on board the *Lydia*, but not go below deck. In the meantime, a mob of angry Bostonians had appeared at the dock. Frightened by the mob, the tax agents ran off without collecting their taxes.

The incident on the *Lydia* was the first time a man of influence had stood up to the laws on taxation. The people of Boston admired Hancock for doing so. As he drove through town in his carriage, people would cheer for him and call him "King" Hancock. To his fellow citizens, John was a symbol of resistance. Most wealthy men living in Boston in the 1760s were Tories, also called Loyalists, who were supporters of the king. While Hancock would not have considered himself a Tory, neither would he have thought himself a Patriot at this time. For in spite of being a member of the Sons of Liberty, he still believed he was fighting for his rights as an Englishman. He had not yet taken up the cause of independence for the colonies.

About a month after the *Lydia* incident, the British warship *Romney* dropped anchor in Boston Harbor. John's sloop, *Liberty*, was docked at Hancock's Wharf, loading cargoes of tar and whale oil. On June 10, a few days before *Liberty* was to set sail, she was seized for loading cargo without a permit. As she was being towed away, an angry crowd of five hundred people appeared on the wharf.

Protesters rioted in the streets and destroyed the property of the tax agents. Although he did not take part in the rioting and destruction, Hancock was sued. John Adams acted as his lawyer. No one from Boston would speak against Hancock, and eventually the government dropped its charges against him. However, *Liberty* was never returned to him.

For many reasons, the citizens of Boston were close to the boiling point, and it didn't help to have the *Romney* sitting just outside the city. At a town meeting in Old South Church, it was decided that twenty-one men would call on Governor Bernard and ask him to order the *Romney* out of Boston Harbor. Hancock and Samuel Adams were among the delegation that visited the governor in his summer home outside of Boston. Instead of agreeing to the men's demands, the governor sent secret letters to two British officers, General Gage in New York and Admiral Hood in Halifax, asking for additional military assistance to keep order in Boston. "I don't think the Sons of Liberty will defend the town against the King's forces, but their activities are short of madness," he wrote to them.[6]

As tensions increased, Governor Bernard felt he was losing control of Boston. On July 1, 1768, he dissolved the Massachusetts legislature, which included the General Council and the House of Representatives. That September, Hancock and four other men met again with Governor Bernard. At this meeting they asked him to reinstate the legislature. When he refused, the citizens of Boston assembled their own Provincial Court. Ninety-six Massachusetts towns were represented by delegates. Hancock was one of the four delegates from Boston. He believed this was a step in the right direction for Massachusetts, and he was in favor of the Provincial Court. He wrote to his business partner in England: "Everything here has been conducted with the greatest order on the part of the people, and I can't but hope that when things are really known in England, we shall be relieved."[7]

# Philadelphia: The Nation's First Capital

Philadelphia is often referred to as our nation's birthplace because of the many historic events that occurred there. In addition to being the site of the First and Second Continental Congresses, in 1790 Philadelphia also became the first temporary capital of the United States. From 1790 to 1800, the president, the Supreme Court, and both houses of Congress worked in the city while a permanent capital was being built on the banks of the Potomac River.

*City Hall, Philadelphia*

Throughout the ten years that Congress met in Philadelphia, it held its meetings in the newly built City Hall near the State House (now called Independence Hall), where the Declaration of Independence had been written and signed. The House of Representatives gathered on the main floor while the Senate assembled on the second floor. (Today, the Senate is still referred to as the "upper chamber.") George Washington was inaugurated for his second term as president in Philadelphia in 1793; John Adams was inaugurated for the first time in 1797. A home owned by wealthy Continental Congress delegate Robert Morris served as the presidential residence for both George Washington and John Adams and their families. The home, which was located at 526-530 High Street, is no longer standing.

While Philadelphia was its capital, the United States took many significant steps toward becoming a full-fledged nation. The Constitution was drafted, the Bill of Rights was added to it, and the U.S. Mint was established.

Philadelphians were hopeful that the Capital would remain in their city and not relocate to Washington, D.C. However, to honor a compromise with the southern states, the capital officially moved to Washington, D.C., in 1800. Thomas Jefferson became the first president to be inaugurated in Washington on March 4, 1801.

Dorothy Quincy Hancock descended from one of the most prominent Massachusetts families. A few years after John Hancock's death, she married a Captain James Scott, who was a friend of her husband's. Captain Scott died in 1809, and Dolly remained a widow until her death in 1830.

# CHAPTER
# 5

## A Lifelong Patriot

On October 1, 1768, the additional military assistance Governor Bernard had requested arrived when twelve British warships sailed into Boston Harbor and landed at Long Wharf. As Bostonians watched in horror, a parade of infantrymen and artillerymen marched on to Boston Commons. The soldiers were quartered all over the city, which made it easy for the Bostonians to see the redcoats and to encounter them every day.

The governor's refusal to reinstate the legislature in 1768 angered the Boston merchants. On January 1 of the following year, they protested by boycotting all the items taxed by the Townshend Acts. The boycott cost British merchants millions of pounds. In England, the merchants pressured Parliament to repeal the Townshend Acts, which it did in 1770. However, as a symbol of its authority, Parliament did not cancel the tax on tea.

By the beginning of 1770, tensions were running high between the British soldiers and citizens. Minor brawls between residents and sentries were common, and any little scuffle brought out a mob. On March 5, 1770, a crowd of Boston citizens cornered some of the soldiers of the Main Guard on King Street. The Guard took up a position of defense and drew their bayonets and muskets. When someone in the mob knocked a soldier to the ground, shots were fired. Five Boston citizens died. The shooting, which Patriots dubbed the Boston Massacre, enraged all of Massachusetts, as well as the other colonies.

Bostonians grew even angrier at having British soldiers occupy their city, and they wanted them gone. Hancock was asked to lead a group of citizens who called upon Lieutenant Governor Hutchinson to remove the British troops. Eventually they were moved from Boston to Castle William, an island in Boston Harbor.

In 1773, England imposed the Tea Act on the colonies. This law allowed England's East India Tea Company to sell tea to certain agents in the colonies. Their tea could be sold for less than the tea sold by colonial merchants, including Hancock. Like the other acts that came before it, the Tea Act angered the colonists, who organized a boycott of imported tea. In December 1773, three British trade ships, *Dartmouth*, *Beaver*, and *Eleanor*, sailed into Boston Harbor. Each held 114 chests of tea, shipped by the East India Tea Company. The citizens of Boston would not allow the ships to unload the tea, and the Sons of Liberty guarded the docks to be sure none was carried ashore. Thomas Hutchinson, who had replaced Bernard as governor in 1771, would not allow the ships to sail out of Boston Harbor before the colonists paid the tea tax.

Boston and Britain were at a standstill. It was only a matter of time until something drastic happened. On December 16, about one hundred men dressed as Mohawk Indians rowed out in small boats to the three British ships. "Let every man do what is right in his own eyes," Hancock shouted as the disguised men cracked open the chests of tea with their axes.[1] In what is now known as the Boston Tea Party, they dumped 342 chests of tea into Boston Harbor.

England was determined to punish Boston for the destruction of the tea. Parliament placed several restrictions, which the colonists called Intolerable Acts, on the city. The Boston Port Bill, which closed Boston Harbor to both foreign and colonial trade, was passed on June 1, 1774. The bill stated that only after the East India Tea Company had been reimbursed for the tea that had been destroyed— a cost of nearly 10,000 pounds—could Boston Harbor reopen. Most of Boston's citizens were merchants, seamen, or shipbuilders who earned their livelihood from the harbor. Therefore, when the Boston Port Bill went into effect, many people lost their jobs.

England also retaliated by appointing a new governor to oversee the colony of Massachusetts. In 1774, Thomas Gage, a military man who had fought in the French and Indian War, was sent to replace

Governor Hutchinson. Gage dealt harshly with the colonists. He closed the reinstated Massachusetts General Court, but its members continued to meet secretly, and changed its name to the Provincial Congress of Massachusetts. Because it was illegal, the Provincial Congress moved from Salem to Cambridge to Concord so that its members would not be found and arrested.

Patriot leaders from the twelve other colonies felt the time had come to deal with England. In September 1774, the First Continental Congress was held in Philadelphia. Samuel Adams and three other men made up the delegation from Massachusetts. As the first president of the Provincial Congress, Hancock remained behind in Massachusetts. He was also made the head of the Committee of Safety. In this position he was authorized to call out the local militia, the minutemen.

During the events of the early 1770s, Hancock emerged as a strong leader. His speeches stirred his fellow citizens to stand up for their rights against England. Little by little, he was devoting his life, his time, and his money to the cause of independence. His personal life was put aside so that he might be of service to Massachusetts. He was nearly forty years old, and he hadn't yet married.

A young friend of Aunt Lydia's named Dorothy Quincy had been spending a lot of time at the house on Beacon Hill. Dolly, as she was called, was about ten years younger than Hancock. Her ancestors were Puritans who had settled in Hancock's native town of Braintree. Her father and grandfather were judges. Dolly's cousin, Samuel, had attended Harvard with Hancock. Aunt Lydia had decided that Dolly would make a good wife for Hancock, and she was hoping the two would set a wedding date.

However, Hancock, who was often traveling with the Provincial Congress, had little time for romance. In 1775, he had been reelected president of the Congress. By April that year, a proclamation had been issued in London ordering the capture and killing of Hancock, Samuel Adams, and other Patriots of Boston who were thought to be leading the thirteen colonies into rebellion. British soldiers were ordered to "put the above persons immediately to the sword, destroy their houses and plunder their effects. It is just they should be the first victims to the mischiefs they have brought upon us."[2]

Knowing they would be arrested and killed if they returned to Boston, after the close of the Provincial Congress, Hancock and

Samuel Adams went instead to Hancock's grandfather's parsonage in Lexington. Aunt Lydia and Dolly were already there. From Lexington, Hancock and Adams planned to travel as delegates to Philadelphia for the opening of the Second Continental Congress in May.

Meanwhile, Governor Gage had learned that the Provincial Congress had set up a store of weapons in Concord. He sent a regiment of 4,000 soldiers to find them. Paul Revere, a silversmith and a messenger of the Boston Committee of Safety, was dispatched to warn Hancock and Adams. He found the men at the parsonage. As chairman of the Committee of Safety, Hancock ordered the weapons in Concord to be separated and hidden in neighboring villages.

On April 18, 1775, six companies of British soldiers marched on the nearby city of Concord. Their aim was to find the storehouse of weapons and capture the two rebel leaders. The British knew that if the weapons were found and the leaders captured, the rebellion would be stopped before it could even get started. Meanwhile, General Gage offered a pardon to all who had taken part in the rebellion—except Hancock and Adams. When captured, these two rebel ringleaders were to be sent to England for trial, at which they would certainly be found guilty of treason, then sent back to Boston for hanging.

Hancock ordered the alarm sounded in Lexington Commons, and the minutemen began to muster. Intending to stay and fight the British soldiers, Hancock began cleaning his gun. He was, according to Dolly Quincy, ready "to go out to the plain by the meetinghouse, where the battle was, to fight with the men who had collected."[3] Adams and Revere persuaded him to travel a short way to a safe house in Woburn. Still, Hancock protested, saying: "If I had my musket, I would never turn my back on these troops."[4]

Aunt Lydia and Dolly joined Hancock and Adams at the safe house. Dolly was determined to return to Boston to be with her father, but John and Aunt Lydia would not let her go. "You shall not return as long as there is a British bayonet left in Boston," Hancock told her.[5]

Dolly answered, "Recollect, Mr. Hancock. I am not under your authority yet. I shall go . . . to my father's tomorrow."[6] In the end, she was persuaded to stay with Aunt Lydia in Lexington.

Several days later, Hancock and Adams made their way to Hartford, Connecticut, where they once again met up with Aunt Lydia and Dolly. From there the party moved to Fairfield, Connecticut. The two women remained at the house of Thaddeus Burr, a county official. Hancock and Adams continued on their journey to Philadelphia to attend the Second Continental Congress.

Two weeks after Congress assembled in Philadelphia, Peyton Randolph resigned as its president, and Hancock was unanimously chosen to succeed him. As president, Hancock had to settle the many differences between the delegates. Tempers flared as the delegates presented their points of view. On many occasions, Hancock had to keep the peace between the radicals, who wanted independence, and the moderates, who felt the colonies should have their own government in place before making a move.

One of the most pressing orders of business for the Second Continental Congress was to organize an army and name its commander in chief. Hancock most likely wanted this position for himself. Nevertheless, on June 15, 1775, Congress made George Washington commander in chief of the Continental Army.

A month later, members of Congress tried to make peace with England. They sent the Olive Branch Petition to King George III, reasserting their loyalty and asking that the fighting be stopped and negotiations begin. The king rejected Congress's attempt at peace. He declared the colonies to be in open rebellion against the mother country. Congress responded by forming a navy and asking all merchants to turn their trading vessels into warships.

On August 28, 1775, while the Second Continental Congress was on a short break, John and Dolly were married at the Burr home in Fairfield, Connecticut. Aunt Lydia died soon after the wedding. Dolly returned to Philadelphia with Hancock, where she was a model wife, and helped the Congress as a secretary. Her manner impressed John Adams, who told his wife, Abigail, that Dolly Hancock "behaves with modesty, dignity and discretion."[7] The Hancocks had a daughter, Lydia, born in late 1776. She died before she was a year old.

In the spring of 1776, Congress gave General Washington permission to move against the British troops quartered in Boston. Hancock had more at stake than any of the other delegates in Congress. His home, business, real estate holdings, and ships could all be destroyed if the British and Patriots went to battle in Boston. But Hancock was prepared to lose all in the name of freedom. "If the expulsion of the British Army . . . require [Boston] to be burned to ashes, issue the order for that purpose immediately," he said in an address to Congress.[8] However, the Patriots did not need to attack the city. In March of 1776, the British soldiers left Boston on their own. With them went about a thousand Tories, among them some of Dolly's relatives.

After the Declaration of Independence was issued, Hancock remained president of the Continental Congress until October 1777. He then took a leave of absence to return to his home in Beacon Hill. His two and a half years of service to his new country had left him exhausted. In addition, he was suffering from gout. Before leaving, he addressed Congress, saying, "I pray Heaven that unanimity & perseverance may go hand in hand in this house, and that every-thing which may tend to distract or divide your councils be forever banished."[9] Hancock may have been wishing unanimity for himself as well, for over the years his once close relationship with Samuel Adams had deteriorated.

In November 1777, the town of Boston turned out to welcome John and Dolly Hancock back home. While the British had been quartered in Boston, the Hancock home had been used as a general's residence, and later as a hospital. The Hancocks quickly returned it to the way it had been before the war. They opened their home to all Boston citizens: Commoners as well as the wealthy were invited to the many parties and social events held there. A large bowl of punch was made each morning, and delicacies were laid out on a table for anyone who stopped by. Dolly once said that her husband's "hobby was his dinner table."[10]

Hancock lead the Massachusetts Convention when the Articles of Confederation were approved for the state in January 1778. Also, in May 1778, John and Dolly's son, John George Washington Hancock, was born. Toward the end of the same year, John was named a major general in the Massachusetts militia. In the fall of 1778, he led his "New Englanders" into battle in Rhode Island, where they were defeated.

In 1780 Hancock was elected the first governor of the state of Massachusetts. He held the office until 1785, when he became

too ill with gout to fulfill his duties. That same year, he was once again elected president of Congress, but being unable to travel, he resigned his position altogether. Many times during these years he was bedridden or wheelchair-bound. His illness turned him from the friendly, sociable man of his youth to one who was irritable and short-tempered.

In 1787, John George Washington fell while ice skating and died from injuries to his head. While still in mourning, Hancock was once again asked to be the governor of Massachusetts, and he accepted. During the convention held to approve the U.S. Constitution, Hancock urged its passing, but along with Samuel Adams, he wanted to see the individual states have more power than the federal government.

Hancock ran for vice president in April 1789, but lost to his friend and fellow Massachusetts Patriot John Adams. Hancock continued to be elected governor, and he helped Samuel Adams become lieutenant governor. The two men became close again. By this time, Hancock's hands and feet were so swollen with gout that he had to be carried on a litter to meetings and state occasions. At one of the last state meetings over which he presided, he had to give a speech sitting down.

John Hancock died suddenly on October 8, 1793, at the age of fifty-six. His body lay in state in the mansion on Beacon Hill as thousands of people came to pay their respects. His funeral procession included Samuel Adams, who took over as governor after Hancock's death; Vice President John Adams; members of the U.S. Senate and House of Representatives; and Secretary of War Henry Knox.

John Hancock had left orders for a simple funeral and had requested that no gun be fired over his grave. The mansion at Beacon Hill was left to Dolly, who donated it to the town of Boston. Years later, the Massachusetts State House was erected on the Hancock property.

John Hancock once called himself a friend of a government founded on reason and justice.[11] He lived his life as such until his last day. Placing his love of liberty before his business, his home, and his personal life, John Hancock showed all who knew him, and those who learn about him, what it means to be a true Patriot.

## The Articles of Confederation

After years of resisting a strong central government in England, and going to war to be free of it, the citizens of the newly formed United States did not want to give Congress too much control. The Continental Congress that met in 1774 and 1775 couldn't collect taxes, nor could it directly control the states in matters such as recruitment for the Continental Army. After the Declaration of Independence was ratified, the states began to create individual constitutions, and the role of the Congress in their day-to-day operations became better defined. Still, there needed to be guidelines in place defining what part of government would be under the control of Congress, and what would be under the states. This document was called the Articles of Confederation, and by 1781, it had been adopted by all the states.

The Articles of Confederation gave more authority to the individual states and less to a central governmental power. Under the Articles of Confederation, Congress had the authority to conduct foreign affairs, declare war, and staff an army and navy, among other things. But Congress had not the power to oversee other important governmental tasks, such as collect taxes and enforce some laws. Within a short time it became evident to the leaders of the young nation that many activities needed to be performed by Congress.

In 1787, the Constitutional Convention was held in Philadelphia. The Articles of Confederation remained in effect until March 4, 1789, when all the states had ratified the Constitution. Although they were not perfect, the Articles of Confederation served as the first national law of the new United States

The Articles of Confederation made the colonies into states. The Constitution insured that no one branch of the government—executive, legislative, or judicial—would become more powerful than any other. This is the way the United States is governed even today.

# Chapter Notes

## Chapter 1   A Nation Is Born

1. In my research I uncovered several variations of this quote. In some, Hancock refers to George III as "John Bull." I have changed the wording slightly to increase understanding.

2. Frederick Wagner, *Patriot's Choice: The Story of John Hancock* (New York: Dodd, Mead & Company, 1964), p. 151.

3. Ibid.

## Chapter 2   A Future Founding Father

1. Frederick Wagner, *Patriot's Choice: The Story of John Hancock* (New York: Dodd, Mead & Company, 1964), p. 24.

## Chapter 3   The Merchant Prince

1. Lorenzo Sears, *John Hancock: Picturesque Patriot* (Boston: Little, Brown and Company, 1912), p. 69.

2. Frederick Wagner, *Patriot's Choice: The Story of John Hancock* (New York: Dodd, Mead & Company, 1964), p. 42.

3. William M. Fowler, *The Baron of Beacon Hill* (Boston: Houghton Mifflin Company, 1980), p. 42.

4. Sears, p. 49.

5. Wagner, p. 41.

6. Ellen C.D.Q. Woodbury, *Dorothy Quincy: Wife of John Hancock* (New York: The Neal Publishing Company, 1905), p. 28.

7. Wagner, p. 47.

8. Fowler, p. 46.

9. Wagner, p. 54.

10. Ibid., p. 57.

11. Kenneth Umbreit, *Founding Fathers: Men Who Shaped Our Tradition* (Port Washington, NY: Kennikat Press, 1969), p. 168.

12. Woodbury, p. 30.

## Chapter 4   Rebel Ringleader

1. Frederick Wagner, *Patriot's Choice: The Story of John Hancock* (New York: Dodd, Mead & Company, 1964), p. 61.

2. William M. Fowler, *The Baron of Beacon Hill* (Boston: Houghton Mifflin Company, 1980), p. 60.

3. Kenneth Umbreit, *Founding Fathers: Men Who Shaped Our Tradition* (Port Washington, NY: Kennikat Press, 1969), p. 168.

4. Wagner, p. 69.

5. Ibid., p. 67.

6. Paraphrase of Wagner, p. 79.

7. Wagner, p. 79.

## Chapter 5   A Lifelong Patriot

1. Frederick Wagner, *Patriot's Choice: The Story of John Hancock* (New York: Dodd, Mead & Company, 1964), p. 98.

2. Ellen C.D.Q. Woodbury, *Dorothy Quincy: Wife of John Hancock* (New York: The Neal Publishing Company, 1905), p. 53.

3. Wagner, p. 114.

4. Ibid., p. 115.

5. Woodbury, p. 68.

6. Ibid.

7. Wagner, p. 137.

8. Woodbury, p. 102.

9. Wagner, p. 155.

10. Woodbury, p. 186.

11. Paraphrase of Wagner, p. 100.

# Chronology

|  |  |
|---|---|
| **1737** | John Hancock is born on January 23 in Braintree (now Quincy), Massachusetts |
| **1744** | His father dies; he goes to live with Aunt Lydia and Uncle Thomas Hancock in Boston |
| **1754** | Graduates from Harvard on July 17; joins uncle's business |
| **1760–1761** | Lives in London, learning uncle's business |
| **1763** | His uncle makes him a partner in Thomas Hancock & Co. |
| **1764** | His uncle dies |
| **1765** | Joins the Sons of Liberty and writes letters to protest Stamp Act |
| **1768** | Stands up to tax officers who try to board his ship *Lydia*; they are chased away by a Boston mob; the British seize his ship *Liberty* |
| **1775** | Flees Boston with Samuel Adams after King George III puts a price on his head; is named President of the Second Continental Congress; marries Dolly Quincy on August 28; Aunt Lydia dies |
| **1776** | Is the first to sign the Declaration of Independence; daughter, Lydia, is born |
| **1777** | Daughter, Lydia, dies; he retires from Congress |
| **1778** | Son, John George Washington Hancock, is born; John returns to Congress; is part of Massachusetts Convention; is made a major general in the Massachusetts militia |
| **1780** | Is elected the first governor of Massachusetts |
| **1785** | Resigns as governor because of his gout; is elected president of Congress and resigns |
| **1787** | His son dies after a skating accident; is again governor of Massachusetts |
| **1789** | Runs for vice president of the United States but loses to John Adams |
| **1793** | Dies on October 8 |
| **1830** | Dolly Hancock dies |

# Timeline in History

| | |
|---|---|
| **1660** | Parliament passes the first of several Navigation Acts, which discourage the colonies from trading with countries that are not part of the British Empire. |
| **1732** | Georgia becomes the thirteenth colony. |
| **1754–1763** | The French and Indian War is fought. |
| **1760** | George III becomes king. |
| **1764** | Parliament passes the Sugar Act on April 5. |
| **1765** | Parliament passes the Stamp Act on March 22. |
| **1767** | Parliament passes the Townshend Acts on June 29. |
| **1770** | The Boston Massacre occurs on March 5. |
| **1773** | Parliament passes the Tea Act; the Sons of Liberty retaliate by organizing the Boston Tea Party on December 16. |
| **1774** | Parliament passes a series of acts which together are called the Intolerable Acts; the First Continental Congress meets in Philadelphia from September 5 to October 26. |
| **1775** | The Battles of Lexington and Concord are fought on April 19; the Second Continental Congress assembles in Philadelphia on May 10; George Washington is named commander in chief on June 15. |
| **1776** | Thomas Paine publishes "Common Sense" on January 15; the Declaration of Independence is adopted on July 4 and signed on August 2. |
| **1781** | The United States adopts the Articles of Confederation. |
| **1789** | The French Revolution begins. George Washington becomes first president of the United States. |
| **1790** | Rhode Island becomes the thirteenth state when it ratifies the United States Constitution. |
| **1812** | The United States declares war on Great Britain on June 12. |

# Further Reading

## For Young Adults

Brenner, Barbara. *If You Were There in 1776.* New York: Bradbury Press, 1994.

Collier, Christopher, and James Lincoln Collier. *The American Revolution 1763–1783.* Tarrytown, New York: Benchmark Books, 1998.

Fradin, Dennis Brindell. *The Signers: The Fifty-Six Stories Behind the Declaration of Independence.* New York: Walker & Co., 2002.

Koslow, Philip. *John Hancock: A Signature Life.* New York: Franklin Watts, 1998.

Somervill, Barbara A. *John Hancock: Signer for Independence.* Minneapolis: Compass Point Books, 2005.

## Works Consulted

Brandes, Paul D. *John Hancock's Life and Speeches.* Lanham, Maryland: Scarecrow Press, 1996.

Fowler, William M., Jr. *The Baron of Beacon Hill.* Boston: Houghton Mifflin Company, 1980.

Sears, Lorenzo. *John Hancock: Picturesque Patriot.* Boston: Little, Brown and Company, 1912.

Umbreit, Kenneth. *Founding Fathers: Men Who Shaped Our Tradition.* Port Washington, New York: Kennikat Press, 1969.

Unger, Harlow Guiles. *John Hancock: Merchant King and American Patriot.* New York: John Wiley & Sons, Inc., 2000.

Wagner, Frederick. *Patriot's Choice: The Story of John Hancock.* New York: Dodd, Mead & Company, 1964.

Woodbury, Ellen C.D.Q., *Dorothy Quincy: Wife of John Hancock.* New York: The Neal Publishing Company, 1905.

## On the Internet

U.S. History: "John Hancock"
http://www.ushistory.org/declaration/signers/hancock.htm

Colonial Hall: "John Hancock, 1737–1793"
http://www.colonialhall.com/hancock/hancock.php

The National Archives Experience
Includes pictures of the original Declaration of Independence
http://www.archives.gov/national-archives-experience/charters/treasure/index.html

U.S. History: "The Declaration of Independence"
http://www.ushistory.org/declaration

# Glossary

**abstain (ab-STAYN)**
To choose not to do something.

**adjourn (ud-JERN)**
To dismiss a meeting.

**aristocrat (uh-RIS-tuh-krat)**
A member of the upper class.

**credibility (kreh-dih-BIH-lih-tee)**
Being believable.

**effigy (EH-fih-jee)**
A dummy that represents someone who is alive.

**gout (GOWT)**
A disease caused by buildup of uric acid in the body, which forms crystals in the joints and makes them swollen and painful.

**Madeira (muh-DEE-ruh)**
A strong wine.

**manse (MANTS)**
A home in which ministers live while serving a church.

**monopoly (mah-NAH-puh-lee)**
Total control over what can be sold.

**radical (RAA-dih-kul)**
A person who wants to see a change.

**rhetoric (REH-tuh-rik)**
Writing and speaking skills used to convince others of one's opinions.

**unanimity (yoo-nah-NIH-mih-tee)**
Being in agreement.

# Index

Adams, Abigail   39
Adams, John   10, 11, 14, 16, 17, 22, 23, 27, 31, 32, 33, 39, 41
Adams, Samuel   15, 26, 27, 28, 31, 32, 37, 38, 39, 40, 41
Articles of Confederation   40, 42
Bernard, Francis   28, 30, 32, 35, 36
Boston Latin School   15, 16
Boston Massacre   35
Boston Port Bill   25, 36
Boston Tea Party   25, 36
Burr, Thaddeus   39
Declaration of Independence   6, 7, 8–9, 40
Declaratory Act   29
East India Tea Company   36
First Continental Congress   7, 11, 25, 26, 37
Franklin, Benjamin   10, 15
French and Indian War   19, 23, 36
Gage, Thomas   32, 36, 37, 38
General Council   15
George II   13, 20, 21, 22
George III   7, 10, 11, 13, 21, 22, 25, 39
Hancock, Dorothy Quincy "Dolly" (wife)   34, 37, 38, 39, 40, 41
Hancock, Ebenezer (brother)   14, 15
Hancock, John
   attends Harvard   16
   birth of   14
   education of   15
   governor of Massachusetts   40–41
   and *Liberty*   32
   and *Lydia*   31
   marriage of   39
   leads Massachusetts Convention   40
   as president of Second Continental Congress   6, 7, 39
   during Revolutionary War   39–40
   runs for vice president   41

signs Declaration of Independence   6, 7
   joins Sons of Liberty   27
   travels to London   19, 20
Hancock, John (father)   14
Hancock, John George Washington (son)   40
Hancock, Lydia (aunt)   15, 21, 22, 37, 39
Hancock, Lydia (daughter)   39
Hancock, Mary (mother)   14
Hancock, Mary (sister)   14, 15
Hancock, Thomas (uncle)   14, 15, 16, 19, 21, 22
Harvard University   14, 16, 17, 22
Holyoke, Edward   16
Hood   32
Hutchinson, Thomas   28, 36
Intolerable Acts   25, 36
Jefferson, Thomas   8–9, 10, 33
Kensington Gardens   20
Knox, Henry   41
Long Room Club   24
Olive Branch Petition   39
Oliver, Andrew   28
Palace of Westminster   29
Pennsylvania State House   7, 8, 33
Pownall, Thomas   18, 19
Quincy, Dorothy (*see* Hancock, Dorothy Quincy)
Quincy, Samuel   16, 37
Randolph, Peyton   39
Revere, Paul   38
Second Continental Congress   7–9, 11, 26, 38, 39
Sons of Liberty   27, 28, 30, 32, 36
Stamp Act   24, 27, 28–30
Sugar Act   23–24, 31
Tea Act   36
Thomson, Charles   9
Townshend Acts   31, 35
Washington, D.C.   33
Washington, George   8, 9, 11, 33, 39